Prodigal

MICHAEL HURD

A cantata in popular style
for unison voices (with divisions) and piano
with guitar chord symbols

Novello Publishing Limited

8–9 Frith Street, London W1V 5TZ

Commissioned by the South Australian Public Schools Music Society
for the 1989 Festival of Music, Adelaide, 4-12 September. Revised April 1991.

Visit the Music Sales Internet Music Shop
at http://www.musicsales.co.uk

Exclusive distributors:
Music Sales Limited, Newmarket Road
Bury St Edmunds, Suffolk IP33 3YB
All rights reserved.

Order No. NOV200206 ISBN 0-85360-675-7
© Copyright 1996 Novello & Company Limited.

Music set by Stave Origination.
Cover illustration by Belle Mellor
Cover design by Jon Forss
Printed in the United Kingdom by
Caligraving Limited, Thetford, Norfolk.

PRODIGAL

Words & music by
MICHAEL HURD

1

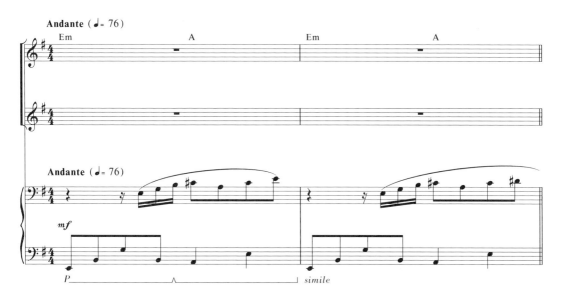

1. Ma-ny years a - go In a coun-try far a-way There lived a weal - thy
2. It was not to be. Things were not to work out quite Ac - cord - ing to the

4

5

2

Allegro moderato (♩=120)

1. I want to go to the big bad ci - ty, Want to go where the lights are bright.
(2.) lis - ten to your ob - ject-ions, You can keep all your good ad - vice.

I want to go where the girls are pret - ty And there's plen - ty of fun at night.
And as for vot - ing in the e - lect - ions, I won't do it at an - y price.

I want to go where the grass is green - er And there's no-thing to do but play.
I kiss good-bye to my civ - ic du - ties. I won't list - en to what you say.

I want to go to the big bad ci - ty And I'm pack-ing my bags to
And tho' you reg - is - ter your ob - ject - ions I will

3

Andante con moto (♩=88)

1. In the ci - ty, free and ea - sy,
2. He was proud and he was haugh - ty.

Doo - be - doo.

Andante con moto (♩=88)

Ev - en though the life was slea - zy, He in - sis - ted he was hav - ing a good time.
Frank - ly, he was ra - ther naugh - ty, Yet it seemed that he was hav - ing a good time.

Doo - be, doo - be - doo. Doo - be, doo - be. Be - doo - be,

B9   B7   E7   E7   A

He had learned the lin - go And knew ex - act - ly what to say. And then he start - ed
Nev - er ev - en no - ticed That he was grow - ing ve - ry poor. Oh he was fool - ish,

Be - doo - be, Doo - be - doo - be, doo - be, doo - be. Doo - be -

E7-9   A7   D   Dm6   A   Bm   E7

back - ing hor - ses, Did - n't stop to count his loss - es, 'Nev - er mind', he said 'I'm hav - ing a
he was sil - ly. Go - ing down hill, wil - ly - nil - ly. Com - ing to the end of hav - ing a

- doo. Doo - be - doo - be. Doo - be, doo - be, doo - be.

1
A   Dm6   A   Bm7   E7   E7aug   A   **2**

ter - rib - ly good good time.'
ter - rib - ly good good   time.

Doo - be, doo - be - doo.   - doo.

4

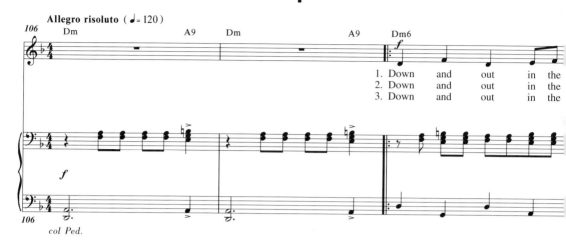

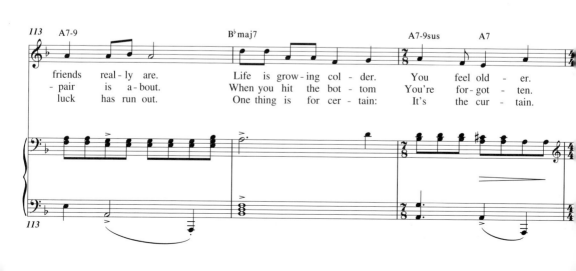

The life you've led has cut you down to size.___ You thought you played it pret-ty
It's far too late to try and make a-mends.___ You can't un-do the things you've
There is no fu-ture now you've lost your friends.___ From now it's down-hill all the

And now at last you're forced to re - a-lize You've been a
The trou-ble you are fac-ing nev - er ends It's just be-
This is the mo-ment when the mu - sic ends And you must

cool.
done.
way.

fool.
- gun.

pay.

14

5

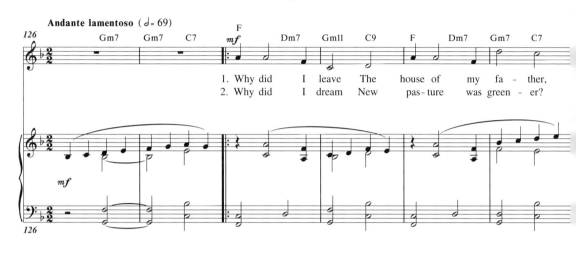

1. Why did I leave The house of my fa - ther,
2. Why did I dream New pas - ture was green - er?

Heed - less - ly throw - ing The fu - ture a - way? Why did I squan - der
Why did I think it was Bet - ter than old? Why did I seek The

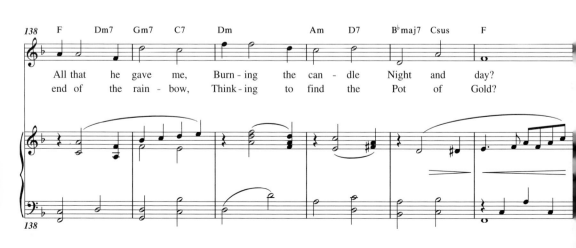

All that he gave me, Burn - ing the can - dle Night and day?
end of the rain - bow, Think - ing to find the Pot of Gold?

15

16

Spoken (solo voice): But his father did not reject him. He knew the prodigal had learned his lesson and that a new life would begin for them all:

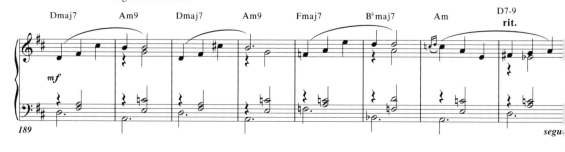

segu

7

20

8

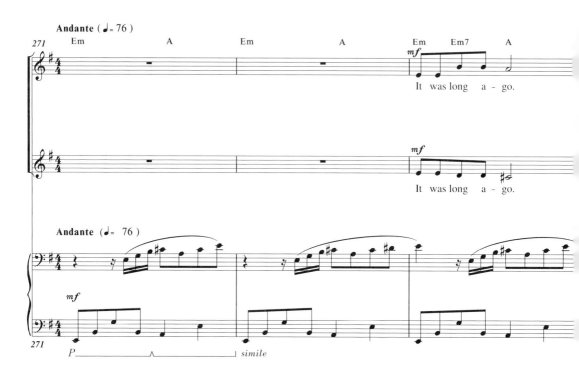

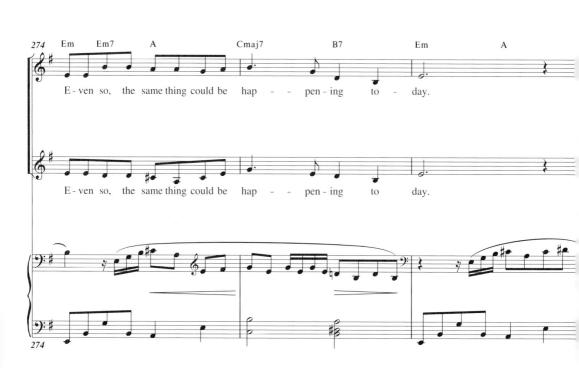